Name in Queensland Modern Cursive
The greatest show on Earth.
AF585283

CONTENTS

INTRODUCTION

The current Queensland handwriting script was introduced over several years from 1985, after a successful trial. Its print style, the Beginner's Alphabet, is based on simple, italic cursive shapes that are easily joined to become Queensland Modern Cursive. Because capitals remain the same, the two scripts merge easily, so children find cursive writing much easier to write as well as read. Queensland Modern Cursive is designed to be fluent and quick, with maximum legibility.

FOCUS

This book contains a carefully sequenced, thorough handwriting program for children in Year 3:

- commencement of writing on 4 mm red and blue lines
- revision of cursive elements on single letters (joins train reference card included)
- progressive joining of cursive letters from two-letter combinations to short words and sentences
- Tracing of both large and smaller examples to internalise correct letter shape and direction
- slope
- fun activities with letters and writing patterns.
- Theme: the circus.

TECHNIQUE

Pencil grip

1. The thumb and the index finger support the pencil while it rests on the middle finger.
2. Child should be able to tap the pencil with the pointer finger while it is supported by the middle finger and thumb.
3. There should be a distance of approx. 2–2.5 cm from the pencil point to the tip of the index finger, 3 cm for a left-hander. Triangular pencil-grips promote correct finger placement and distance.

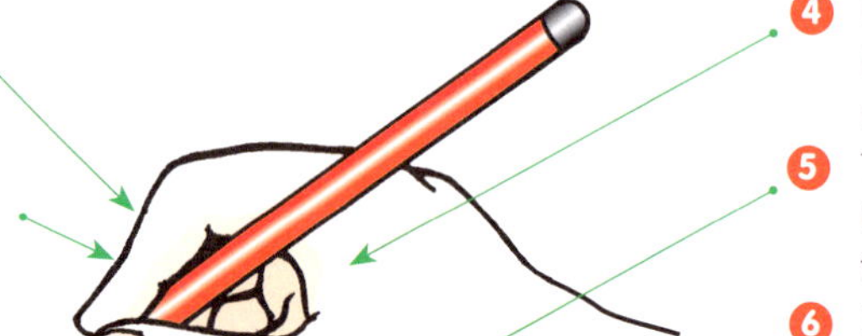

4. Hold pencil barrel up high, near or before the knuckle. Pencil should not rest low in the "web" of the hand.
5. The side of the hand and the little finger act as supports for the whole hand.
6. Unpainted pencils are less slippery.

Posture

Right-handers

1. Keep back straight at an angle of about 30° to back of chair, and keep bottom towards back of seat.
2. Make sure that book or paper is sufficient distance from the edge of the desk to enable most/all of the forearm to rest on the desk. Move book up as child works down the page to maintain this.
3. Table or desk height about level with child's waistline or a bit higher. The weight of the body is supported by the non-writing arm.
4. Sloping desks are ideal, especially for struggling writers.
5. Feet should be flat on the floor.

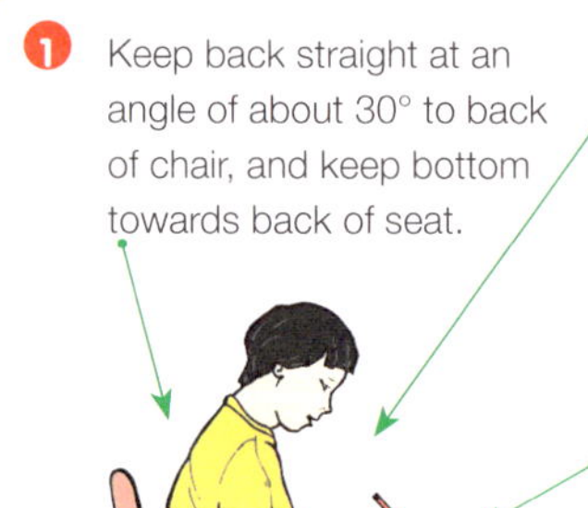

Left-handers

Left-handers should have their elbow in to discourage a hooked wrist.

Posture rhyme:

1, 2, 3, 4. Are your feet flat on the floor?
5, 6, 7, 8. Is your back nice and straight?
9, 10, 11, 12. Show me how your pencil's held.
13, 14, 15, 16. Slope your book to do your writing.

Paper Position

Left-handed

Right-handed

Right-handed

GENERAL TEACHING TIPS

- Purchase extra copies of *Write for Queensland*—Book 3 and *Write for Queensland*—Book 2 (remedial work) to laminate for non-permanent marker use, allowing incidental, all-year reinforcement of handwriting lessons.
- Display joins train and the cursive alphabet across the top of the board.
- Contact joins trains to children's desks.
- Modelling on the board or an overhead screen one word at a time assists internalisation of letter and join shape and direction.
- Slope should be encouraged at this stage.
- Soft HB pencils (unpainted) are recommended for later stages.

Please see further information on the learning features of this book on page 3 and Teacher's Notes on page 63.

LEARNING FEATURES

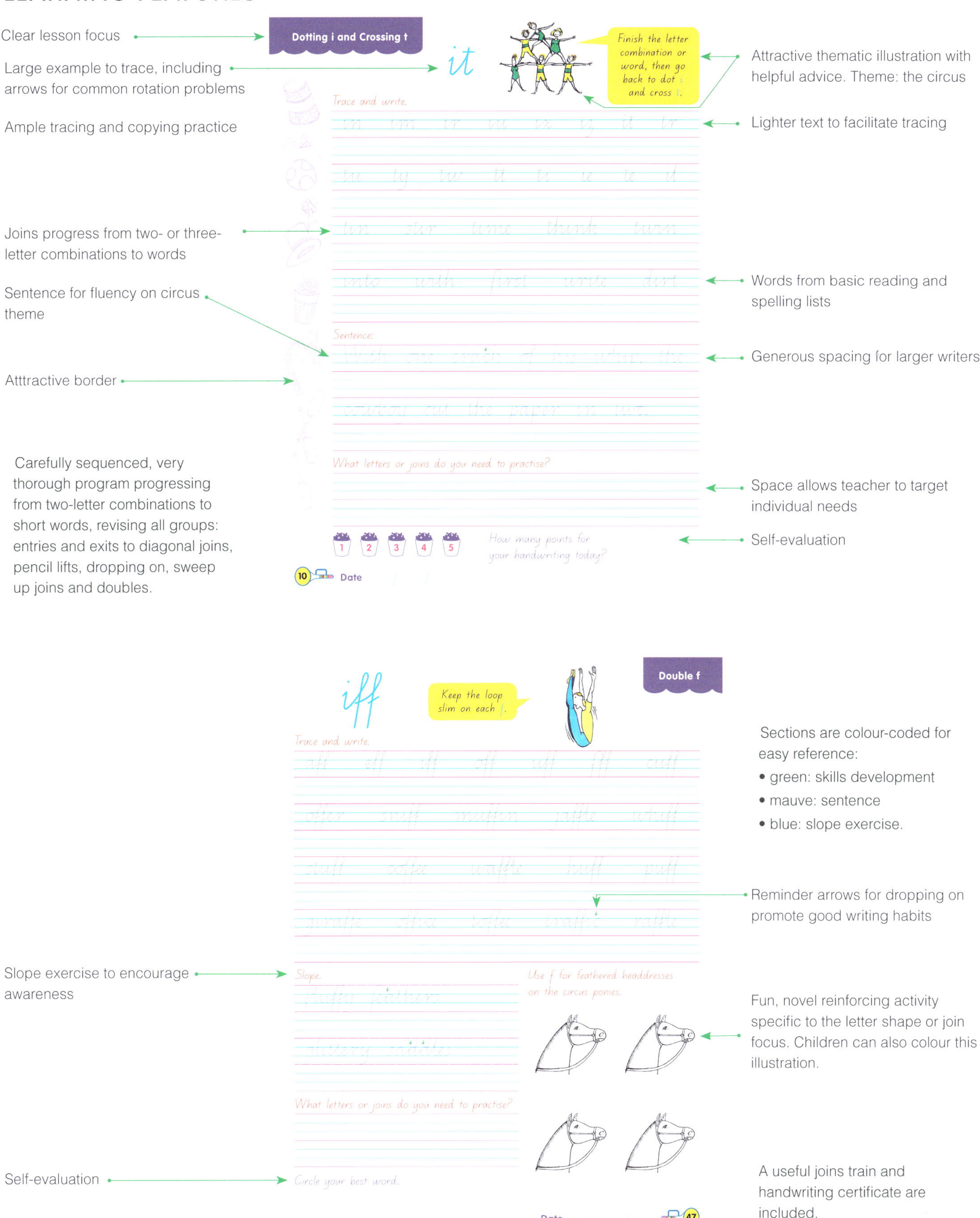

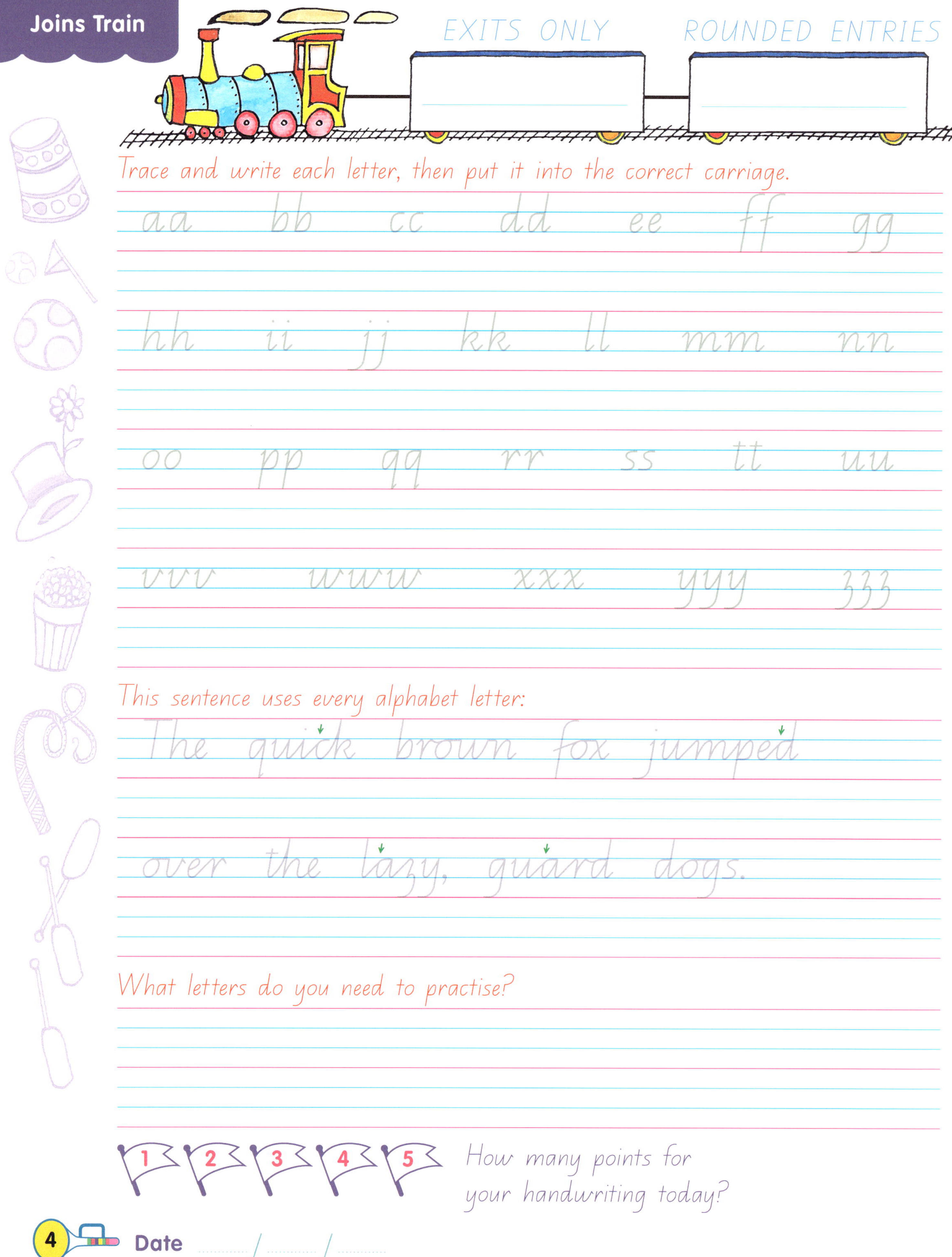

Trace and write each letter, then put it into the correct carriage.

aa bb cc dd ee ff gg

hh ii jj kk ll mm nn

oo pp qq rr ss tt uu

vvv www xxx yyy zzz

This sentence uses every alphabet letter:

The quick brown fox jumped

over the lazy, guard dogs.

What letters do you need to practise?

1 2 3 4 5 How many points for your handwriting today?

Date .... / .... / ....

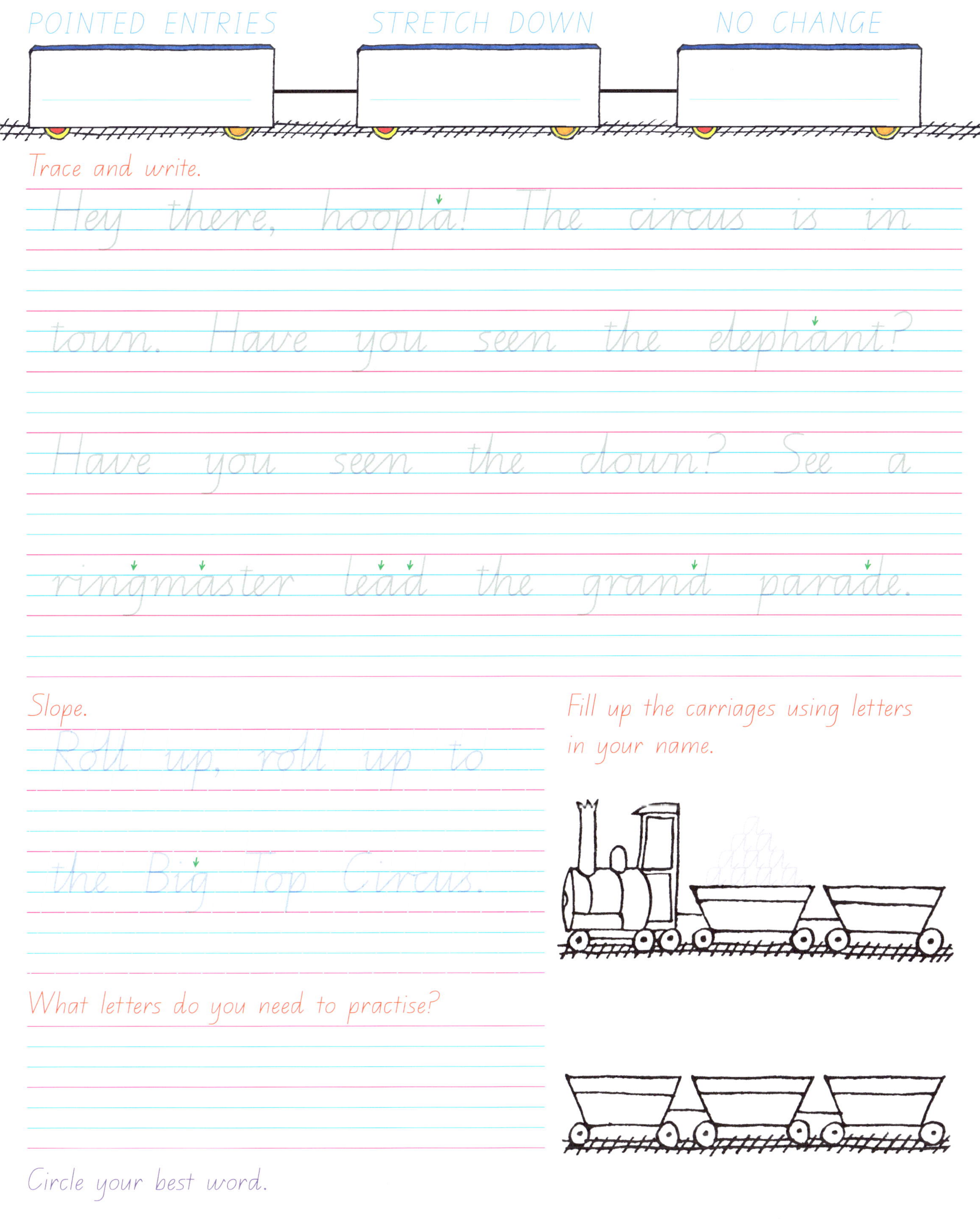

POINTED ENTRIES

STRETCH DOWN

NO CHANGE

Trace and write.

Hey there, hooplà! The circus is in

town. Have you seen the elephant?

Have you seen the clown? See a

ringmaster lead the grand parade.

Slope.

Roll up, roll up to

the Big Top Circus.

What letters do you need to practise?

Fill up the carriages using letters in your name.

Circle your best word.

Date .... / .... / ....

Exits to Pointed Entries —i, j, p, u, v, w, y

ai

Trace and write.

ai ci di ei hi ki li mi

ti ni ui au cu du hu mu

but cup my city hut lip

kite five two key new hip

Sentence:

The funny clown runs around,

his baggy pants falling down.

What letters do you need to practise?

How many points for your handwriting today?

Date .... / .... / ....

ev

Stretch out to separate letters.

Trace and write.

lu du nu hu ay cy dy my ey

ny ly ev ew av aw ap ep up

step hit any jaw fun ever

tip sip nut tin say live

Slope.

tiny monkey bike

whip cracking

What letters or joins do you need to practise?

Write the printed letters in a different colour over the cursive.

ni

Circle your best pair.

Date ____ / ____ / ____

an

Make sure your rounded entries look different from your pointed entries.

Trace and write.

an am ar en em er un um

ur cr tr dr lm kr dr en

pan are ten hen her sun

Tim mum him cry art ant

Sentence:

The daring rider jumped on his bike through a ring of fire.

What letters or joins do you need to practise?

How many points for your handwriting today?

Date ...... / ...... / ......

With x, do the exit before you cross it. Drop on the next letter, any letter.

Trace and write.

ax ax ax ax ex ex ex ex

ix ix ix ix ux ux ux ux

six axe axle mix next sixty

x-ray fix tax text sax except

Slope.

axe throwing act

sixty hula hoops

What letters do you need to practise?

Write the printed letters in a different colour over the cursive.

e n

Circle your best x.

Date / /

Finish the letter combination or word, then go back to dot i and cross t.

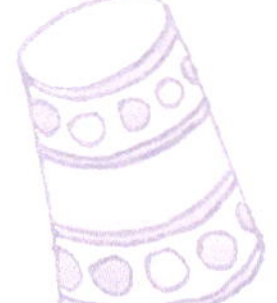

Trace and write.

in im ir iu ix iz it tr

tu ty tw tt ti ie te il

tin stir time think twin

into with first write dirt

Sentence:

With one crack of his whip, the cowboy cut the paper in two.

What letters or joins do you need to practise?

How many points for your handwriting today?

Date .... / .... / ....

ne

Stretch out the exit at the angle of a slippery-slide to start letter e.

Trace and write.

ae ce de ee he ie ke le te

ne me ue see been the mine

feet tent sleep seen few deep

men blue nine help week three

Slope.

snakecharm flute

ten metre climb

Use the e pattern to give the clown curly hair.

What letters or joins do you need to practise?

Circle your best diagonal join.

Date .... / .... / ....

Cross f upwards to join onto the next letter.

Trace and write.

fee fire food fry few fine

full for from fly feet first

fun four front floor feed five

Sentence:

Can Fonzo lift fifty-five kilos?

Drumroll. Fonzo did it! Bravo!

What letters or joins do you need to practise?

How many points for your handwriting today?

Date .... / .... / ....

az

Letter z finishes flat on the line like g, j and y.

Trace and write.

az az az az ez ez ez ez

iz iz iz iz uz uz uz uz

buzz fizz jazz sizzle dizzy

puzzle pizza crazy quiz guzzle

Slope.

weight-lifting prize

strong muscle-man

Fill the weights with coloured letters f and z.

What letters or joins do you need to practise?

Circle your best diagonal join.

Date .... / .... / ....

Three letters—no lifting until the end of the word.

Trace and write.

any her den die kin lip

mix key new cup mum lie

fix tip fir dim hen aim

men due kit hip let fit

Sentence:

Watch the trapeze artists swing

and twirl above the safety net.

What letters or joins do you need to practise?

How many points for your handwriting today?

Date .... / .... / ....

Stretch out between letters at the angle of a slippery slide for easy-to-read writing.

Trace and write.

dew fin the hem din few

eel ate nun tux fee duo

meet tent lump net nine

line tune time fine keep

Slope.

ladies and gentlemen

boys and girls

Draw a ladder and child on each extra-long exit.

a c e

i u n

m x k

What letters or joins do you need to practise?

Circle your best join.

Date ____ / ____ / ____

qu

Trace and write.

quick quiet quiz queen

quack quite quit quad

quartz quilt quail queue

question quiet quarter quokka

Sentence:

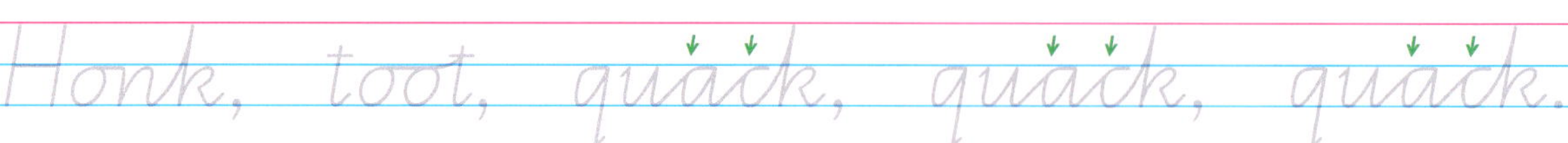

Honk, toot, quack, quack, quack.

Write your full name in capitals, twice.

How many points for your handwriting today?

Letter o joins easily without lifting. Go up to the top centre of o, then back and around. No lifting.

Trace and write.

ao co do eo fo ho lo io ko

mo no to uo boat does hot

lost lion knot most tow done

slow before cold block smoke photo

Slope.

Cleo, Toto and Rocko;

dogs in frilly skirts.

What letters do you need to practise?

Circle your best join to o.

Use capitals to fill in the gaps.

THE GREAT

__________ CIRCUS

IS COMING TO

____

SEE THE

____

____

____

BE THERE!

COST __________

Date .... / .... / ....

Sweep Up Joins to Tall Letters —b, h, k, l, t

Curve up to the top of tall letters. Don't lift your pencil.

Trace and write.

ab ah al ak at ib il ik it

ch ck eb el et ub uh ul th

kite chip pink like they back

help them about make bike

Sentence:

A cloud of black smoke came

out of the clown's tiny red car.

What letters or joins do you need to practise?

How many points for your handwriting today?

Date 

Lift after Clockwise Finishers —b, y

If a letter finishes in this direction, it doesn't join.

Trace and write.

been yum but your bell yell

keys buy bite type blue dye

blew eyes bent yard bump

baby always able ball bubble

Slope.

I can juggle balls,

rings and plates.

What letters or joins do you need to practise?

Complete the circus ring using colours. Draw a performing juggler.

bybybyby

Circle your best word.

Date / /

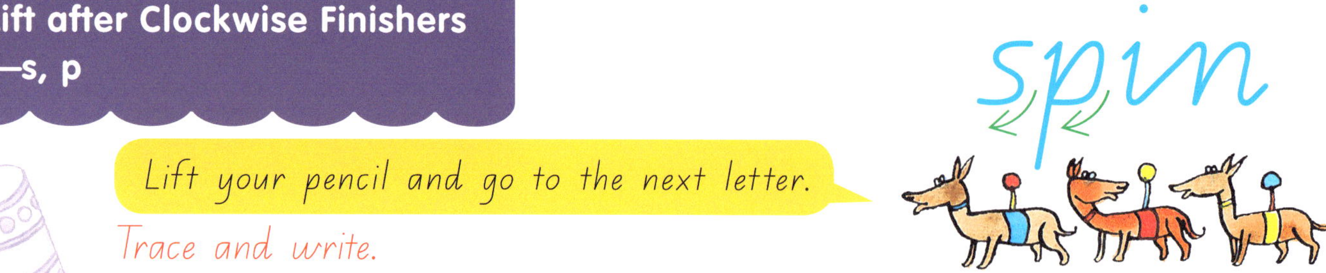

Lift your pencil and go to the next letter.

Trace and write.

say pet six pin sat pip

pup sit pull sail pen salt

pay saw pat seem pie sell

plum ship paper sleep puppy

Sentence:

See three poodles stand on their hind legs, twirl and jump around.

What letters or joins do you need to practise?

How many points for your handwriting today?

 Date .... / .... / ....

jugs

Lift after Clockwise Finishers —j, g, z

Any letter that finishes flat doesn't join.

Trace and write.

jet game zip jaw glue gap

zap jam page jar edge buzz

jelly gym size jump fizzy

jeep pizza jazz bigger puzzle

Slope.

The trio of lions yawned lazily.

What letters or joins do you need to practise?

Circle your best word.

Complete the circus ring using colours. Draw a trained dog act.

Date ..... / ..... / .....

Drop On to High Exits—a, c

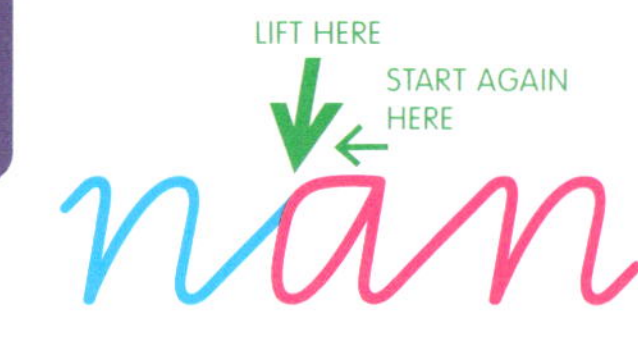

Bring the exit up high to the top blue line, then write the shoulder, or flat top, to meet it. Don't copy the arrows.

Trace and write, using colours.

n nan m man t tan l lap

a act i ice h ham c cat d day

car pick fat back call eat

much dear many name play

Sentence:

Elephants, seals, dogs in hats,

strong men, jugglers, acrobats.

What letters or joins do you need to practise?

How many points for your handwriting today?

Date .... / .... / ....

A high exit at a slippery slide angle separates the letters before dropping on.

Trace and write, using colours.

a ago a add e equip e edge

said age aqua bad leg and

begin find bag did sing tide

again under eight side things

Slope.

practise each day

balancing act

What letters or joins do you need to practise?

Circle your best drop on.

Decorate the clown's outfit with drop-on letters.

Date / /

Drop On to High Exits —a, c, d, g, q

Trace and write, using colours.

send mice camp pack meal

tick than near lunch page

came make eighty hear place

Sentence:

"Ready—catch!" said the man to eight hungry, clapping seals.

What letters or joins do you need to practise?

How many points for your handwriting today?

Date .... / .... / ....

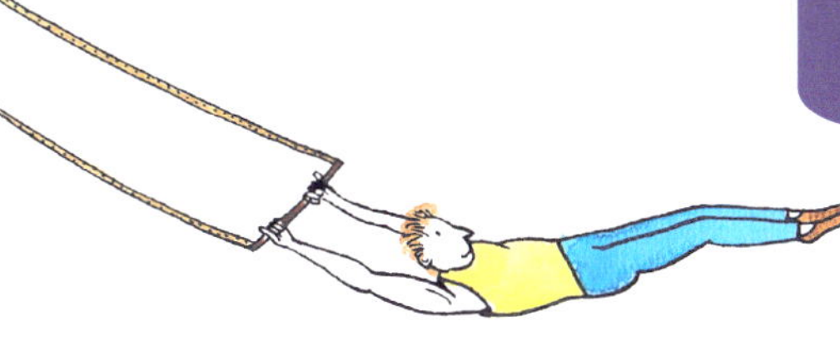

Drop On to High Exits—a, c, d, g, q

Stretch out the exit to the top blue line.

Trace and write, using colours.

nice talk can't small lake

such snake fair date chain

sand shed king heap lamb

child seat night tame thank

Slope.

magician's hat

Abracadabra!

Give each letter an extra long exit and ladder. Draw a child on each.

v e u

m x h

k t i

What letters or joins do you need to practise?

Circle your best drop on.

Date / /

Make rainbow writing by changing colour at every arrow.

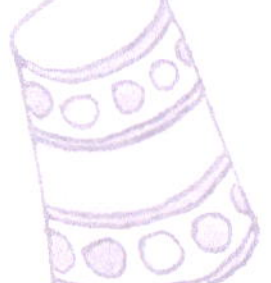

Trace and write, using colours.

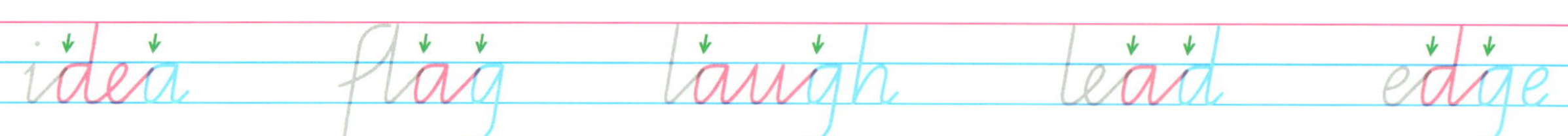

head each hand made lady

idea flag laugh lead edge

beach place special land cage

magic danger ladder candle

Sentence:

Maddy the Magician dazzled all. Now for his final trick.

What letters or joins do you need to practise?

How many points for your handwriting today?

Date .... / .... / ....

Touch the top blue line before changing colour.

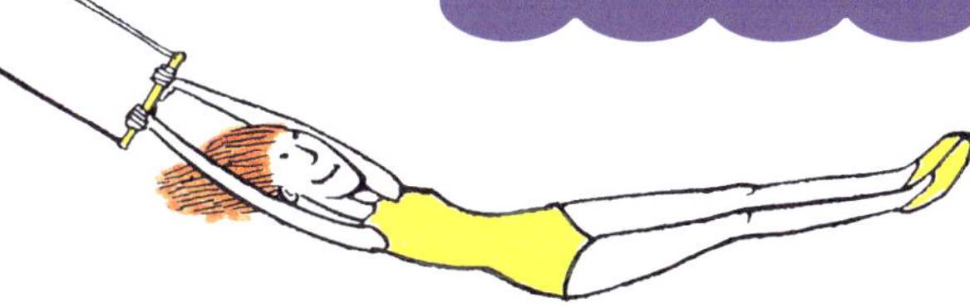

Trace and write, using colours.

nana tack picnic peach

place black change naughty

catch shade accept teacher

Sunday daddy candy dead

Slope.

acrobat handstands

face-painting lady

Drop on c to put skirts on the dancing bears.

What letters or joins do you need to practise?

Circle your best word.

Letters that finish near the top go straight across the blue line to the next letter. Don't lift your pencil.

Trace and write.

oa oi oc od on om or op

ou ov ow ox oy oz oo og

you stop come only how toy

too dog onto four know today

Sentence:

Watch the india-rubber woman

tie her arms and legs in knots.

What letters or joins do you need to practise?

How many points for your handwriting today?

Date .... / .... / ....

The downstroke on v and w now goes straight across the blue line. Don't lift your pencil.

Trace and write.

va vi vu vo vy wa wi wr

wu wn wy will news wig

vine with view want water

away swim walk wind two

Slope.

swirling ribbons

chair balancer

What letters or joins do you need to practise?

Use colours and the u pattern to finish the rug.

Circle your best horizontal join.

Date .... / .... / ....

ri

ri ri ra ra ru ru rn rn

rs rs rp rp ro ro ry ry

arm first run sharp rice try

trip rain hairy burn right

Sentence:

The human cannon ball will do the ultimate leap of terror.

What letters or joins do you need to practise?

How many points for your handwriting today?

Date .... / .... / ....

Finish the downstroke of r, then curve up to the next letter.

Trace and write.

from rope horse dry doors

room drop write rose corn

crowd warm down frost tries

brown word bring farm curry

Slope.

Blasting through the air. More, more!

Use the dipping movement from r to fill the box with curly popcorn.

popcorn

What letters or joins do you need to practise?

Circle your best joins from r and from o.

Date ...... / ...... / ......

Avoid a droopy join to e—lift your pencil after o, r, v, w.

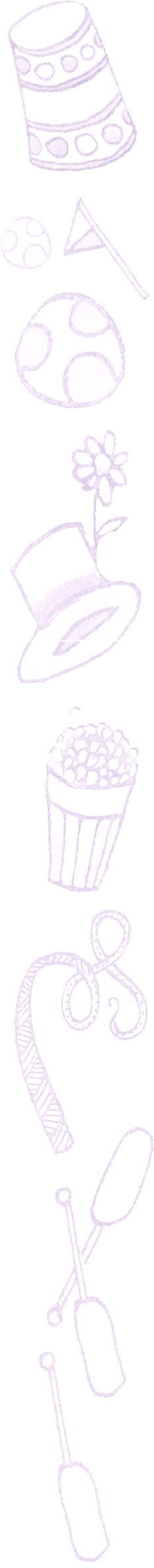

eoe ere eve ewe eoe ere eve ewe

three five every green twenty

went fire very red here shoe

over give were week more read

Sentence:

See twelve, tumbling acrobats

roll over, under, up and down.

What letters or joins do you need to practise?

How many points for your handwriting today?

Date .... / .... / ....

Curve up to the top of tall letters. Don't lift your pencil.

Trace and write.

ob oh ol ok ot of rh rb

rk rt rl rf wh wl wk wt

who wok spot park lolly dirt

world rhyme cob when slowly

Slope.

mobile caravan city

careful fire-eater

Use the sweep up curve to put stripes on the big top. Colour them.

What letters or joins do you need to practise?

Circle your best join to h and b.

Date .... / .... / ....

Consolidation Words

Stretch out between letters for easy-to-read writing.

Trace and write.

then really cool thirty white

alive school seven where story

draw coco-pops okay turn never

forty other sweet growl metre

Sentence:

When the flute played, the cobra swayed out of the cane basket.

What letters or joins do you need to practise?

How many points for your handwriting today?

Date .... / .... / ....

Good posture means good writing!

Trace and write.

litre wrote colour shark great

love which moon centre photo

doctor threw bread post motor

topsy-turvy street corner flower

Slope.

This is the greatest show on Earth.

Finish the basket pattern. Draw a dancing snake with zigzag patterns.

What letters or joins do you need to practise?

Circle your best word.

Date / /

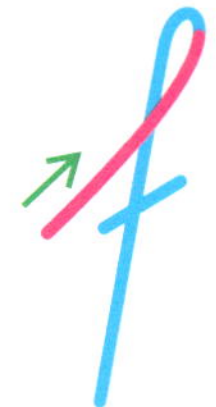

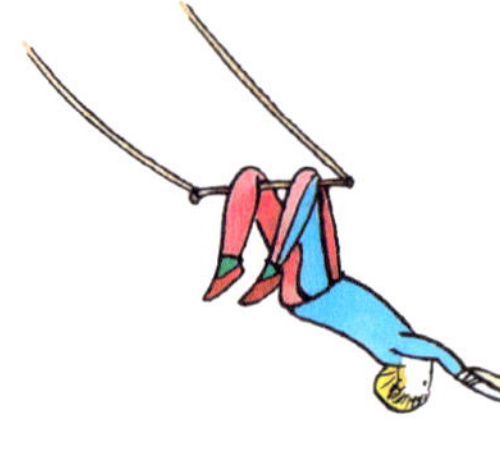

Add a long join to the front of f only when needed.

Trace and write.

af af ef ef if if uf of of lf

afar left life raft soft leaf

fifty self wife often half safe

before golf after afraid fifth

Sentence:

The dare-devil will now perform

another risky motorbike stunt.

What letters or joins do you need to practise?

How many points for your handwriting today?

Date .... / .... / ....

There are two types of letter f. The shoulder on f causes a loop.

Trace and write.

faf fef fif fof fuf faf fef fif fof

loaf calf beef lift knife

wolf gift cafe surf awful

raft roof fifteen myself dwarf

Slope.

performing bikes

perfect backflip

What letters or joins do you need to practise?

Use f with a join to prepare the bike-ramp. Draw a rider.

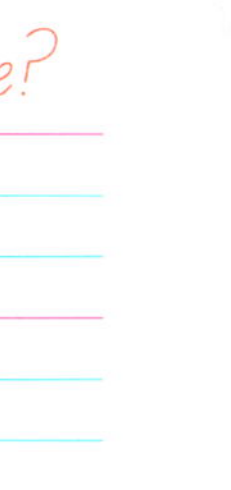

Circle your best f.

Date / /

as as

Cut the shoulder off s after a diagonal join. This is "modified s" or "s with a join".

Join full s, then s without the shoulder.

as as es es is is us us ls ls

ask yes his busy rest also this

fast house must please beside

easy test last fish these push

Sentence:

Silence, please. Enricho curled his trunk and lifted Rosa up high.

What letters do you need to practise?

How many points for your handwriting today?

Date .... / .... / ....

s

Use printed s at the beginning of a word, after o, r, v, w, and after a pencil lift.

Trace and write.

sister socks shoes swims says

stars sails shells snakes lost

stones seeds sticks stories Mars

season jaws sense skips first

Slope.

bears, lions, tigers,

horses and monkeys

Use s waves to give the lion his mane.

What letters or joins do you need to practise?

Circle your best printed s and modified s.

Date / /

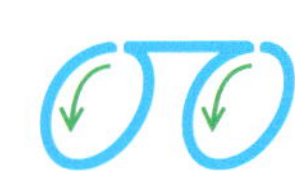

Finish each o in the centre at the top. Don't lift your pencil.

Trace and write.

oooo oooo oooo oooo oooo oooo

cook poor hook woof floor

loose tooth blood choose spoon

The Great Choo-Choo will dive into a shallow pool of water.

What letters or joins do you need to practise?

How many points for your handwriting today?

Date .... / .... / ....

ee

Stretch out between letters for legible writing.

Trace and write.

seen week been deep feet trees

geese queen sheep green cheese

wheel knee meet teeth between

thirteen freeze teeny-weeny beetle

Slope.

one-wheel unicycle

helium balloons

What letters or joins do you need to practise?

Use the e pattern to take the cords to the microphones.

eeee

eeee

eeee

eeee

Circle your best double e.

Date / /

s

Use printed s at the beginning of a word.

Trace and write.

some said shall sent sleep

stop swim shop sing story

shout stone start spoon stick

smile sport soft sure stars

Sentence:

Suzette the Sensational will swallow seven sharp swords.

What letters or joins do you need to practise?

1 2 3 4 5

How many points for your handwriting today?

Date .... / .... / ....

s

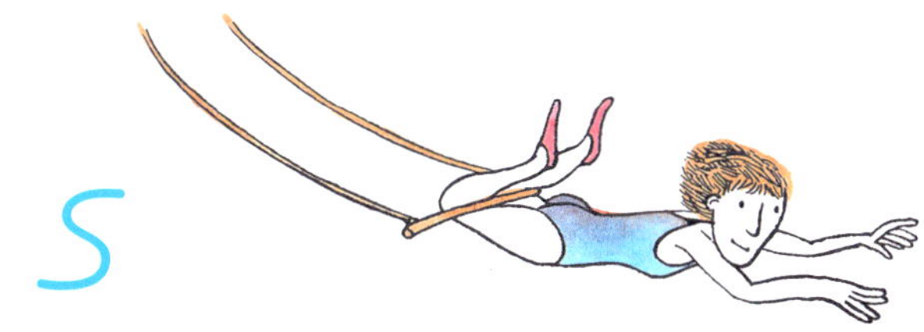

Use printed s after a pencil lift.

Trace and write.

myself plays who's jobs eggs

that's days keeps lambs shops

always where's cups keys upset

belongs it's legs stays things

Slope.

showbags on sale

ringside seats

Cover the clown's outfit with colourful s patterns.

What letters or joins do you need to practise?

Circle your best word in capitals.

Date / /

os

Use printed s after a horizontal join. Don't lift your pencil.

Trace and write.

os rs ws os rs ws os rs ws

hose ours draws most horse

paws close nurse jaws those

Thursday post person yourself

Sentence:

Bears in cars, clowns on bikes,

girls on horses, boys on trikes.

What letters do you need to practise?

1 2 3 4 5 How many points for your handwriting today?

 Date / /

io

When o is the last letter in a word, it finishes at the top.

Trace and write.

no do to two too ago into

who also zero milo hello

silo onto shoo bingo polo

video piano tomato potato

Slope.

Have a photo taken with a lion cub.

Use the o pattern to draw the audience.

What letters do you need to practise?

Circle your best word.

Date .... / .... / ....

Letter f without a Join

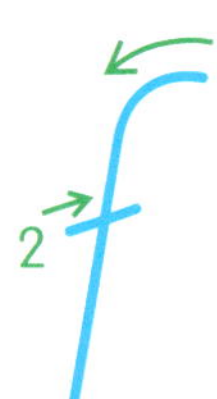

After a pencil lift, go to the top of f.

Trace and write.

ff ff ff ff ff ff ff ff ff

forty-five bagful helpful jugful

twenty-four playful crayfish

boyfriend cupful transfer joyful

Sentence:

Now for a real show-stopper:

Felix, the fearless flame-twirler.

What letters do you need to practise?

How many points for your handwriting today?

Date .... / .... / ....

Keep the loop slim on each f.

Trace and write.

aff eff iff off uff fff cuff

offer sniff muffin jaffle whiff

stuff coffee waffle huff puff

giraffe office toffee traffic raffle

Slope.

fluffy feathers

glittery saddles

Use f for feathered headdresses on the circus ponies.

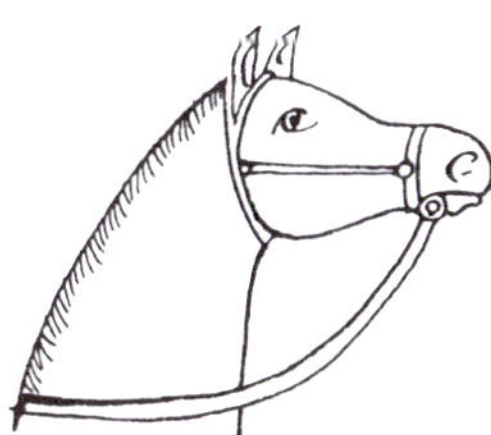

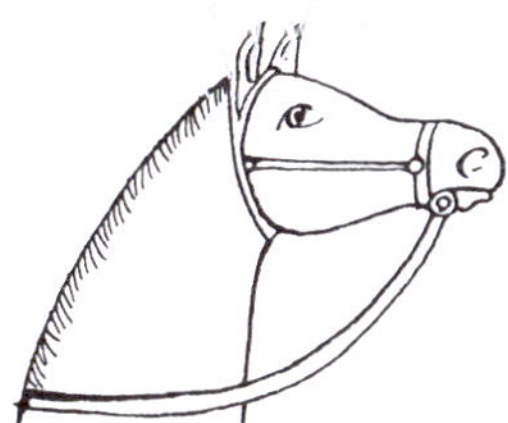

What letters or joins do you need to practise?

Circle your best word.

Date ____ / ____ / ____

Sweep Up Join from f to Tall Letters

Use the crossbar of f to join. Curve up. Don't lift your pencil.

Trace and write.

fly floor flour flew flies

flood flap float flock flow

flag fluffy flame flat flash

flea flower flick flight flip

Sentence:

Crowds flock to see the star of the show, Fifi, fly high above them.

What letters or joins do you need to practise?

How many points for your handwriting today?

Date ....../....../......

ilk

Curve up twice without lifting your pencil.

Trace and write.

milk bulb other elbow colt after

left mother father title chalk

brother little whistle melt stilts

talk another shelter shelf path

Slope.

One whistle — swing.

Two whistles — leap.

Use oooo to knit a safety net for the trapeze artists.

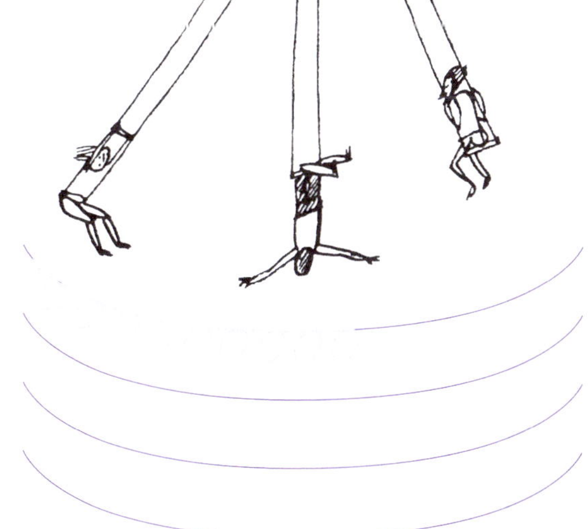

What letters do you need to practise?

Circle your best word.

Date / /

rr or rr

Dip after each r to finish it before joining. Lift if it is too hard.

Try joining double r, then lifting for each r.

arr err irr orr urr arr err irr

curry sorry carrot furry

mirror marry berry terrible

worry arrow tomorrow cherry

Sentence:

Get your ticket for the train, ferris-wheel, or merry-go-round.

What letters or joins do you need to practise?

1 2 3 4 5

How many points for your handwriting today?

Date / /

Give x a high exit, cross it, then the next letter can be dropped on.

Trace and write.

axe taxi boxes extra mixture

sixty-six exit foxes next fixing

exam index exact pixie extinct

exercise waxy toxic oxygen galaxy

Slope.

Pixie, Dixie and Max

got into a down taxi.

Make colourful collars. Finish one x before starting the next.

xxxx

What letters or joins do you need to practise?

Circle your best x.

Date ....../....../......

Stretch the join between double m for legibility. Each m has two wedges.

Trace and write.

amm emm imm omm umm

Emma tummy swimming

hammer mummy common

dummy Summer drumming

Sentence:

The lights dimmed. The drums rolled. Out came the tiger trainer.

What letters or joins do you need to practise?

How many points for your handwriting today?

Date .... / .... / ....

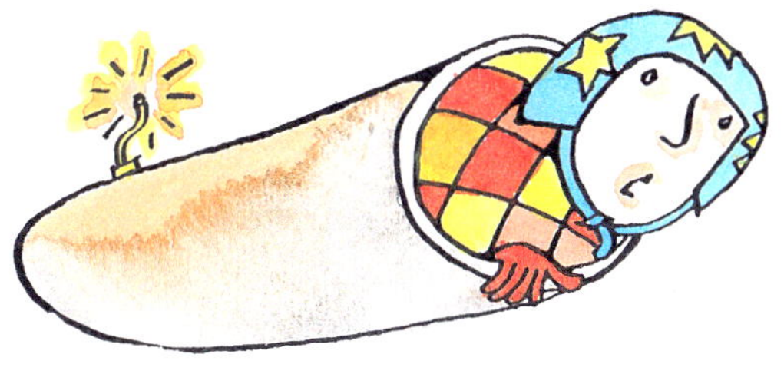

Stretch the join between double n for legibility. Each n has one wedge.

Trace and write.

ann enn inn onn unn

running goanna cannot

nanny manners channel

funny tonnes beginning

Slope.

bunny from a hat

tiger commands

Write the printed letters in a different colour over the cursive.

d i n n e r

What letters or joins do you need to practise?

Circle your best word.

Date / /

Curve up to the top of tall letters. Don't lift your pencil.

Trace and write.

all ell ill oll ull ball full

well spill dolls pull really

jelly bully pillow follow dollar

spelling million gorilla swallow

Sentence:

Nimble Nelly carefully balanced on the rope with an umbrella.

What letters or joins do you need to practise?

How many points for your handwriting today?

Date .... / .... / ....

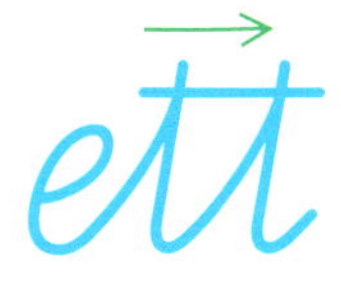

Double t can be crossed with one line.

Trace and write.

att ett itt ott utt otter utter

butter letter kitten bottle little

jetty getting hotter lettuce rattle

pitter-patter spaghetti babysitter

Slope.

Make each letter t into a striped umbrella for a tightrope walker.

What letters or joins do you need to practise?

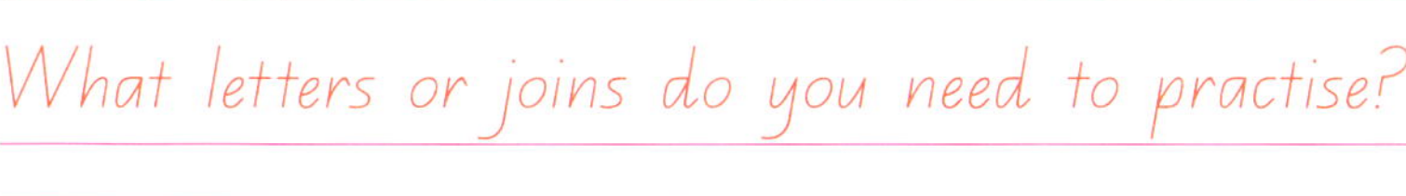

Circle your best double t.

Date ____ / ____ / ____

Double s should look like identical twins.

Trace and write.

ass ess iss uss ass ess iss uss

class guess kiss fuss glass

dress miss puss mass mess

hiss fussy scissors dessert

Sentence:

A big brass band for stomping feet.

Feel the rhythm. Clap that beat.

What letters or joins do you need to practise?

How many points for your handwriting today?

Date ..../......../........

Double s should look like identical twins.

Trace and write.

oss oss oss oss oss oss oss

boss loss moss toss cross

fossil losses possum floss

gross crossing glossy across

Slope.

Intermission drinks,

fairy floss, lollies

What letters or joins do you need to practise?

Circle your best word.

Use the letter s to put paper wrappers on these lollies.

Date ____ / ____ / ____

r ran

Finish r with a flick, then drop on a, c, d, g or q.

Trace and write, using colours.

ran bird yard draw forget

rain circle word tray grass

train circus brave March torch

burger energy brain straw third

Sentence:

Prancing, snorting ponies gallop and trot, canter then stop.

What letters or joins do you need to practise?

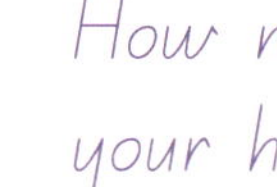

How many points for your handwriting today?

Date .... / .... / ....

r rce

Finish r with a flick, then drop on a, c, d, g or q.

Trace and write, using colours.

crash draw order track

wrap hard afraid large

rake church third travel

garden library word card

Slope.

Marching grand

parade, hooray!

What letters or joins do you need to practise?

Drop on c to put skirts on the dancing bears.

Circle your best word.

Date / /

A careful writer is a neat writer.

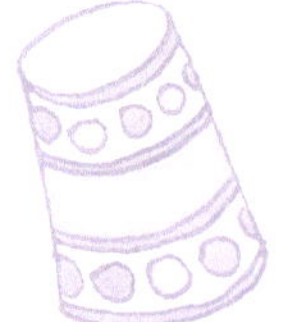

Trace and write.

real push lunch first think

summer work milk down

children while year please

morning today yellow room

Sentence:

The impressed audience clapped and cheered. Bravo, bravo! More!

What letters or joins do you need to practise?

How many points for your handwriting today?

Date .... / .... / ....

Trace and write.

around know hurry seed

because happy seven father

dinner ready inside after off

next zero better possess own

Slope.

So long. Farewell.

Tell your friends.

Finish the rows of seats for the audience.

What letters do you need to practise?

Circle your best word.

Date ....../....../......

Trace and write.

Nitro, Mitzi, Za-Za, Fudzwallop,

Mervin the Magnificent, Elfonzo the

Great, Beautiful Babette, Lady Lola,

Naro the Nimble, Dino the Daring

Think of circus names for yourself and some friends.

What acts would you perform?

Date 

TEACHER'S NOTES

Short, daily handwriting lessons are far better than longer, infrequent lessons. Teacher modelling of lesson material on the board to demonstrate the flow of handwriting is essential.

Page

1 Title page and list of contents

2 Introduction

3 Learning Features of Book 3

4 As a class, write each letter, then work out which carriage it belongs in. I have used the term "stretch down", meaning cursive "f" and "z" are longer than in their printed forms. See reference card on inside back cover.

7 Superimposing the printed forms of letters over the cursive assists children having difficulty reading cursive.

12 The crossbar of "f" is flexible. It is lower when joining to "e" and higher when joining from a top finisher.

15 It is useful to liken the angle of a diagonal join to that of a slippery-slide to assist correct spacing between letters.

16 "Pencil lift" describes a deliberate stopping within a cursive word and restarting at the beginning of the next letter to continue that word. It promotes fluency, speed and legibility by avoiding slow, messy looping.

17 The small gap in the large "o" is to ensure children write it with the correct rotation. Do not copy it. All capitals remain printed and separate.

18 A "covering stroke" occurs when there is a retracing back down part of the ascenders. No lifting.

19 Clockwise finishers are letters that finish on the left-hand side of their form and do not lend themselves to joining. Simply go to the start of the next letter and continue writing.

22 Letters with "shoulders" or flat tops along the top blue line are dropped on to avoid a retracing or rocking motion over and back at the top of them. Dropping on is best after a diagonal join to these letters. All drop on letters are based on the "a" shape. An arrow is used to indicate where the exit stops and dropping on is required, throughout the *Write for Queensland* series. Do not copy the arrows. Changing colour is for novelty value.

28 Horizontal joins occur after letters that finish on or near the top blue line: top finishers "o", "r", "v", and "w". The join goes straight across, or dips slightly in the case of "r", to the next letter. See note for page 17.

30 Ensure "r" finishes wholly with its downstroke before joining horizontally, so that it is not lost. Very uncoordinated writers or poor readers of cursive writing may need to lift after every "r", not before, for legiblility.

32 Top finishers don't join to "e", as this does not allow for the correct position of the loop on letter "e". See note for page 17.

33 Ensure "r" finishes wholly with its downstroke before sweeping up to the ascender, so that it is not lost. See note for page 17.

36–7 Adding a diagonal join before "f" enables it to be joined to. For great understanding of why "f" has a loop, whereas "b", "h", "k" and "l" do not, show "f without a join" in one colour, adding the diagonal join to the start of "f" in another colour: the shoulder, or flat top, on "f" necessitates the loop. When not joining from another letter, "f without a join" is used, i.e. at the beginning of a word and after a capital or clockwise finisher.

38–9, 42–4 After a diagonal join, the flat beginning or shoulder of the "s" disappears, leaving a point. "Modified s" or "s with a join" should look pointed rather than rounded to prevent "s–o" confusion. The base of the "s" remains flat. Printed "s" may also be called "s without a join". It is used at the beginning of a word, after a pencil lift such as following a clockwise finisher or capital, or from a horizontal join. See note for page 17.

40 See note for page 17.

45 See note for page 17.

46–7 Adding a diagonal join before "f" enables it to be joined to. For great understanding of why "f" has a loop, whereas "b", "h", "k" and "l" do not, show "f without a join" in one colour, adding the diagonal join to the start of "f" in another colour: the shoulder, or flat top, on "f" necessitates the loop. When not joining from another letter, "f without a join" is used, i.e. at the beginning of a word and after a capital or clockwise finisher.

48 The crossbar of "f" is flexible. It is lower when joining to "e" and higher when joining from a top finisher. When there is no join to "f", start at the top of its form.

48–9 A "covering stroke" occurs when there is a retracing back down part of the ascenders. No lifting.

50 Ensure "r" finishes wholly with its downstroke before joining horizontally, so that it is not lost. Very uncoordinated writers or poor readers of cursive writing may need to lift after every "r", not before, for legibility.

54–5 A "covering stroke" occurs when there is a retracing back down part of the ascenders. No lifting.

56–7 After a diagonal join, the flat beginning or shoulder of the "s" disappears, leaving a point. "Modified s" or "s with a join" should look pointed rather than rounded to prevent "s–o" confusion. The base of the "s" remains flat. Printed "s" may also be called "s without a join". It is used at the beginning of a word, after a pencil lift such as following a clockwise finisher or capital, or from a horizontal join.

58–9 The dip/flicking after "r" lends itself to dropping on. This is optional and no reminder arrows are given for this in the *Write for Queensland* series.

62 All capitals remain printed and separate. All capitals start on the top red line.

63 Teacher's Notes

64 Write the child's name in cursive. Self/teacher assessment required. A space is provided for positive aspects to be recorded.

Inside back cover — Reference Card—May be detached and contacted to the student's desk.

Pen Skill Award

has worked hard
on handwriting

Assess your own handwriting.

Rounded Entries:	Very Good	Good	Need Practice
Pointed Entries:	Very Good	Good	Need Practice
Diagonal Joins:	Very Good	Good	Need Practice
Horizontal Joins:	Very Good	Good	Need Practice
Dropping On:	Very Good	Good	Need Practice

Teacher's Comments: ______________________

Date: ______________ Signed: ______________